Naughty

Nice

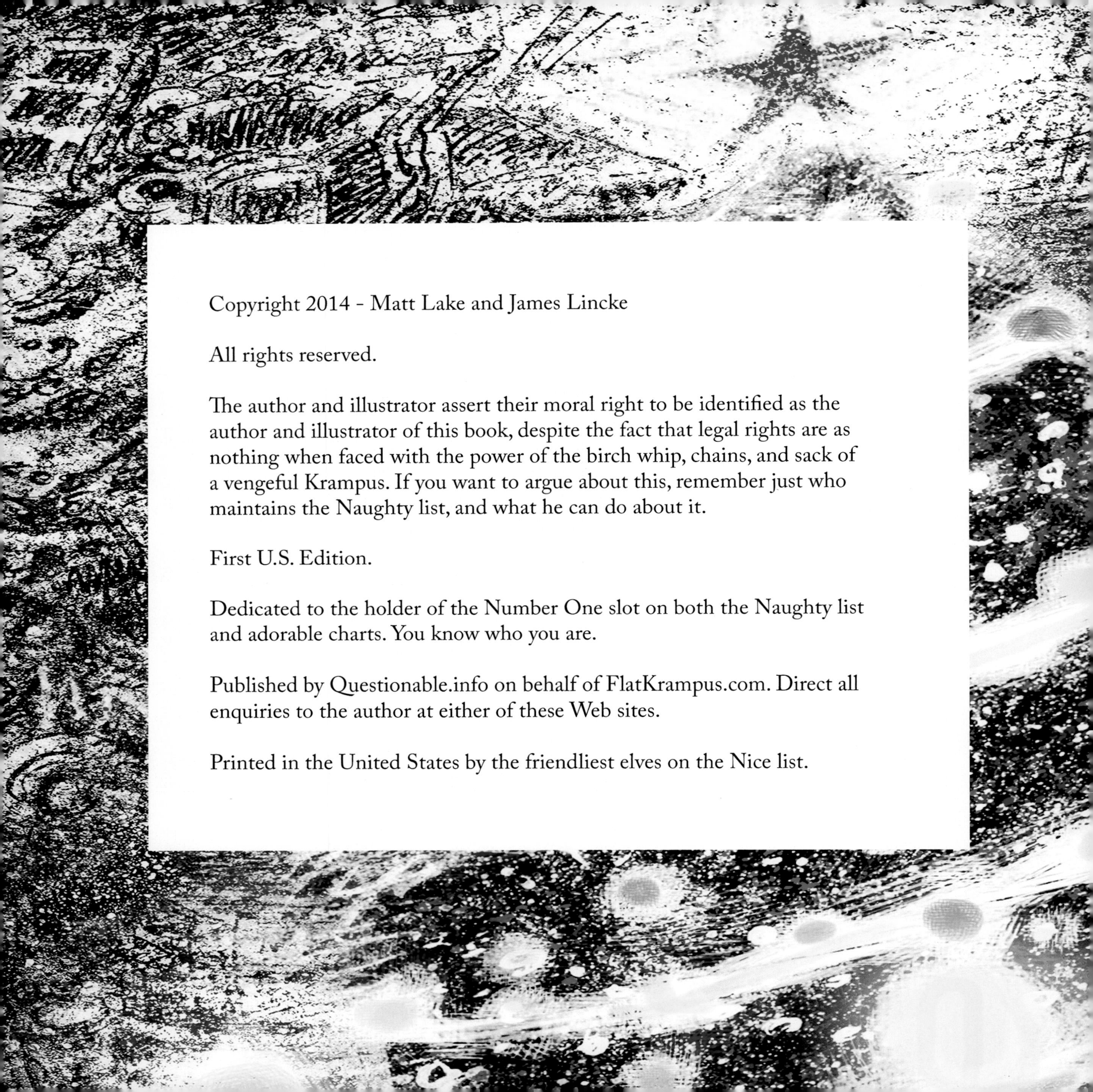

First U.S. Edition.

Dedicated to the holder of the Number One slot on both the Naughty list and adorable charts. You know who you are.

Published by Questionable.info on behalf of FlatKrampus.com. Direct all enquiries to the author at either of these Web sites.

Printed in the United States by the friendliest elves on the Nice list.

Before we get started this evening, please turn to the first carol in your hymn book, *Oh Run All Ye Faithful*, and let us sing together all three verses.

1. Oh Run All Ye Faithful

ADESTE FIDELES | **JOHN F. WADE AND FLAT KRAMPUS**

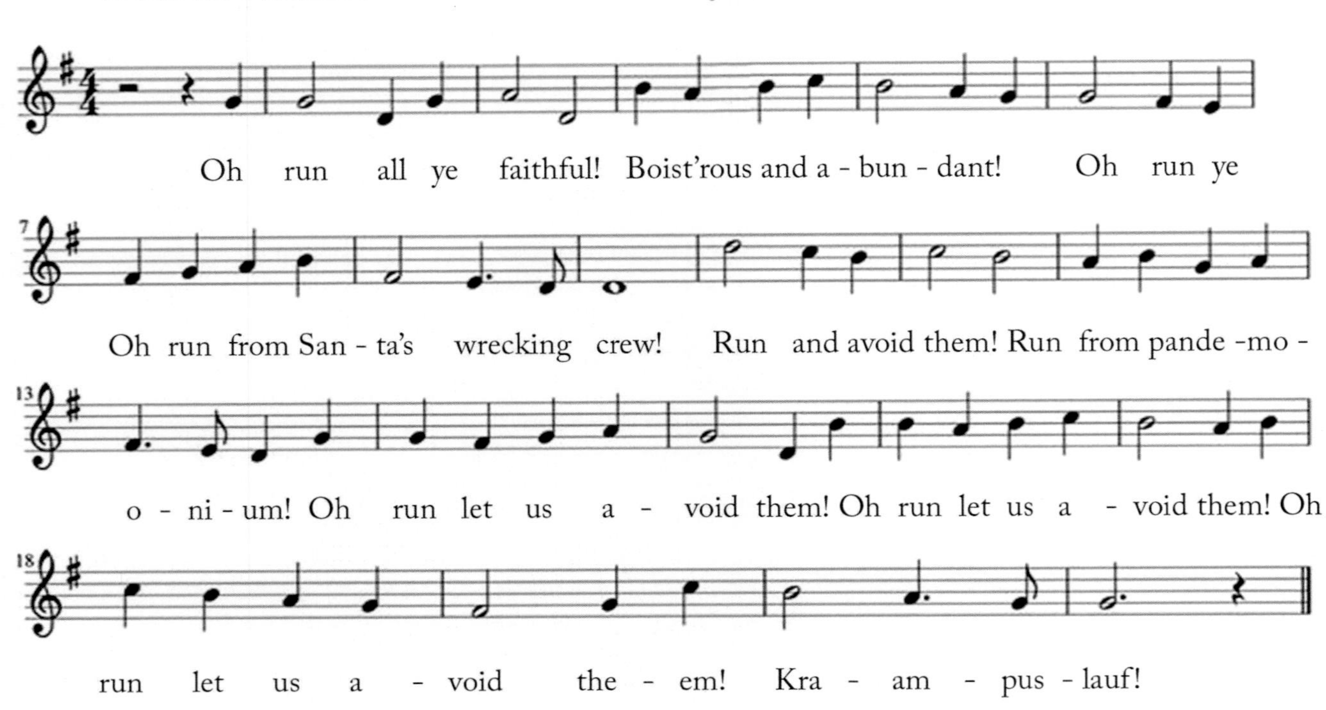

2. Here comes the Krampus! Here comes La Befana!
Here comes the Belznickel to scare you away!
Run and avoid them! Run from pandemonium!
Oh run! Let us avoid them!
Oh run! Let us avoid them!
Oh run! Let us avoid them!
Krampuslauf!

3. Flee from Frau Perchta! Flee in desperation!
Flee Knecht Ruprecht and Zwarte Piet!
Run and avoid them! Run from pandemonium!
Oh run! Let us avoid them!
Oh run! Let us avoid them!
Oh run! Let us avoid them!
Krampuslauf!

Good evening. My name is Santa Claus, and I am the keeper of Christmas cheer. It is my job to remind people to have a good time every winter.

It can be a hard job.

That is why I have a whole cast of characters to help me. Many of you won't know these characters or the customs they celebrate, so let me introduce you to some of them.

A long time ago, the little German and Austrian children used to leave their boots by the door on December 5th. Why? Because in those days, Saint Nicholas would come by and drop nuts and apples into their boots to spread Christmas cheer.

That's what passed for a good time back in the days before Nintendo.

Once upon a time in Italy, the little children used to get their treats on Twelfth Night, which is nearly two weeks after Christmas, clear into January. But Saint Nick had nothing to do with that celebration: Those gifts came from a witch called La Befana.

And in old countries that don't even exist anymore, a parade of strange creatures would run through town, either delighting the onlookers...or terrifying them. They were called Perchten, and they were led by a magical woman called Frau Perchta.

So you see, Christmas isn't all about Santa and elves. It takes a whole motley crew to keep the spirit of Christmas alive, all across the world.

Tonight, on the Night of the Krampus, we'll be visiting one of my favorite companions We will sing some songs about him. We will read a poem together, And maybe, if we feel festive enough, we will put on furry coats and masks and run through the streets in our very own parade. In the old days, they used to call it a Krampuslauf, which means Krampus run.

But for now, here's a little story and some more songs.

Are you sitting comfortably? Then let's begin...

Halloween's over. Thanksgiving has passed.
The trees and the lights have appeared at last.
In the stores, all the Christmas stuff's out on the shelves—
The tinsel, the snowglobes, the lights, and the elves—

And right about now, it can hardly be missed,
The grown-ups start talking about Santa's list!
"Are you naughty or nice?" they all want to know
And each time that they ask you, anxieties grow.

You try to be nice—or at least, well, you should—
But what do they mean? Because no-one's ALL good!
We all get annoyed and do things we regret—
Even grown-ups—and yet we forgive and forget.

So what about Santa's list—naughty or nice?
Well, I'll tell you, but listen! I won't tell you twice!
This secret has been kept for many a year
Santa just keeps the Nice list—there's no need to fear!

If you're basically good, you will get your reward
If you're rotten right through, then prepare for my horde
For I keep the list of the Naughty, I swear

Yes!

I am the Krampus!
You'd better beware!
I assemble my list from close observation
I spy and I phone-tap with great dedication
You may see me or hear me as I skulk about
And know this about me .... I'm no friendly scout!

You'd better believe that I'm not very nice
I'm making a list and I'm checking it twice
And if you are on it, you'd better beware!
I'll punish you hard, and I won't even care!

So how will you know that you're there on my list?
I'll show you some clues that you'll find hard to miss!
Look around till you see me, up high on the shelf,
And check out my hands to see for yourself.

Am I holding a chain to be used for restraint?
Do you think that that's good? 'Cause it certainly ain't!
I chain up the mean kids and laugh as they weep,
And scare most of them straight as their parents all sleep!

Am I holding some birch sticks? Well that's even worse!
If I'm holding some birch sticks, them somebody's cursed!
Those sticks will thrash kids who are thoroughly rotten
If you see them, you'll know that I haven't forgotten!

So there are your warnings — the chain and the sticks.
If you see them, you'd better give up your mean tricks!
'Cause a beating's by far not the worst I can do.
Say your prayers, 'cause you don't want this happening to you!

If you look round your house on a cold winter's day
And I'm up on your shelf, or your couch, or duvet
Look around or behind me, in front and in back,
And see if I've brought my big Krampussy sack

If I have, you're in danger because you've been awful
And punishment's coming that's cruel, but it's lawful,
You'll be stuffed in that sack (it's so sad to tell)
And I'll carry you off in it, straight down to ...

Well!

I think you're now wise to my place in the world
I'm the Krampus! I know every boy and each girl.
Most of you, Santa will shower with love.
The rest of you suffer the Krampus's shove!

So every year, on Saint Nicholas Night
I'll come to your home, not to give you a fright!
But remind you that I keep the naughty kids' list
And no on who's on it will ever be missed.
They'll be gone! And I think that is all for the best.
For peace upon earth, and goodwill to the rest!

Dear Editor—
I am 8 years old. Some of my little friends say there is no Krampus. Papa says, "If you can find it written somewhere, it must be so." Please tell me the truth in writing, is there a Krampus?
—Virginia O'Begon

Virginia, your little friends are wrong. They have been lulled by the materialism of a greedy age into thinking that their wish list is Santa's command. They think that Christmas and life itself is at its best when they have their own way, and nothing else matters. It is sad to say that they will have a rude awakening when they find out the truth. In this great universe of ours, human beings are not kings who may demand tribute, without gratitude or appreciation. Each man and woman, boy and girl, is one of many creatures who must share with those around them, getting what they need, of course, but not expecting to have everything they see and want.

Yes, Virginia, there is a Krampus. He exists as certainly as justice and caring exist, and you know how they are all around us, making our lives secure and our minds easy. How dreadful the world would be if there were no Krampus! It would be as dreadful as if there were no Santa Claus. There would be no childlike sense of fair play then, no reward for those who refuse to succumb to selfishness, and no just retribution for those who do. We should have no enjoyment, except in what we can collect for ourselves. In short, we would have only our possessions to give our lives purpose.

Not believe in Krampus! You might as well not believe in Santa Claus. Your papa might scan the media all day and all night, and might recruit an army of people to do the same all across the world, to search for evidence that the Krampus exists. And if he should not appear before them, what would that prove? Nothing! You cannot see justice with your eyes, easing the victims of wrongdoing. You cannot see a change of heart inside a nasty and bitter person. You cannot see the invisible hand of altruism, nudging people away from those first early acts of selfishness that lead people along the path of meanness. But if you could, you would see the hand of the Krampus—yes, and his whip and chain and burlap sack—pointing the way.

No Krampus? No way in heaven or on earth! Thank God he lives and will live forever. Virginia, if you should live to be a thousand years old, you would find the Krampus continuing his solitary mission of righting wrongs. A thousand years from now—no, even more that that: 10 times 10,000 years from now—he will continue to make children realize that crime does not pay, that cruelty shall not go unpunished, and that doing unto others as you would have them do unto you is the only way we can leave the world a better place than we found it.

KRAMPUS CAROLS

ANCIENT AND MODERN

2. Krampuses Are Coming

WORDS MATT LAKE

2. They see you when you're sleeping
They know when you're awake
They whack you with a whipping branch
So be good for goodness sake!
O! You better hide out!
Or they'll make you cry
They'll make you pout
I'm telling you why...
Krampuses are coming to town!

3. O Krampuslauf

2. O Krampuslauf! O Krampuslauf!
You make me feel safe...not at all
You shout, attack and threaten me
And with your chain you've got us all
How often during Christmastide
Have Krampuses just whipped my hide?
O Krampuslauf! O Krampuslauf!
You make me feel safe not at all

3. O Krampuslauf!O Krampuslauf!
Your props teach me a lesson
The good times always disappear
The bad times are depressing
Your whips, and chains and canvas sack
Keep me from ever falling back
O Krampuslauf! O Krampuslauf!
Your props teach me a lesson

The Krampuslauf or Krampus run is a traditional parade held on St. Nicholas Eve in which many youths of the town dress as the Krampus and run through town

4. O Krampuslauf

O TANNENBAUM

O Kram - pus - lauf, O Krampus - lauf! Wie töd - lich sind dein' Peit - schen

Wenn du kommst zur Weihnachts - zeit, er - schreck'st du die Süd - deut - schen

Du terr - or - is - i - ert bei Nacht, Die kleine Kinder um-ge - bracht

O Kram - pus - lauf, O Krampus - lauf! Wie töd - lich sind dein' Peit - schen

2. O Krampuslauf O Krampuslauf
Du kannst mir nicht gefallen!
Sie greifen mich um zu bedrohen
Und Ketten anzuschnallen
Wie oft hat mich zur Weihnachtszeit
Ein Krampus wirklich nicht erfreut!
O Krampuslauf O Krampuslauf
Du kannst mir nicht gefallen!

3. O Krampuslauf, O Krampuslauf
Dein Dinge will mich lehren:
Die guten Zeiten verschwinden
Die schlechten wiederkehren
Die Peitsche, Kette, oder Sack
Geb' einen bösen Beigeschmack.
O Krampuslauf, o Krampuslauf
Dein Dinge will mich lehren!

5. Wicked Krampus Folk

ENGLISH TRADITIONAL FOLK TUNE - WORDS BY FLAT KRAMPUS

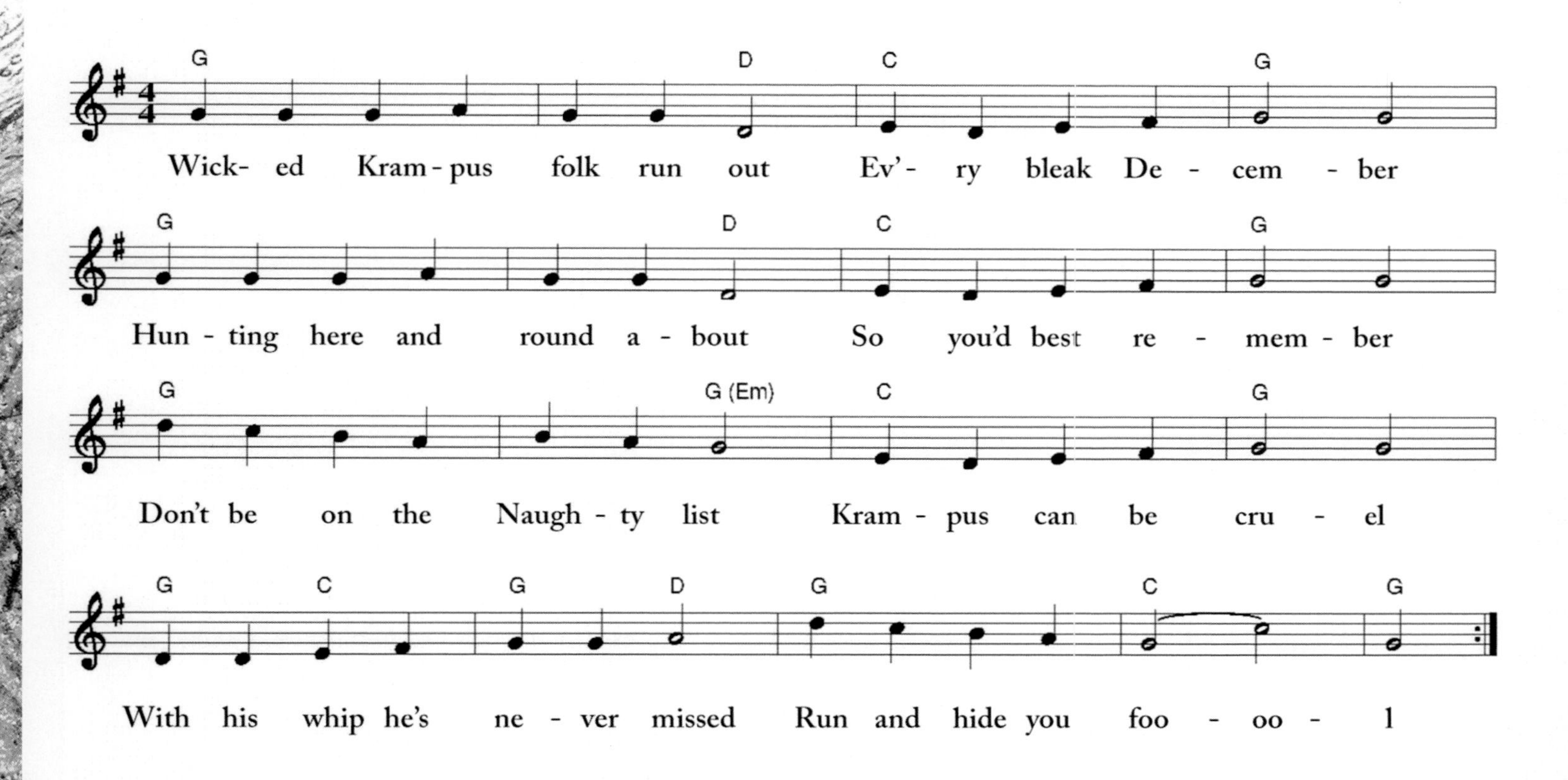

The Twelfth Night of Krampus

On the Twelfth Day of Christmas, the Krampus gave to me:

Twelve peasants howling
Eleven elves a-pouting
Ten lords a-weeping
Nine ladies sobbing
Eight maids a-grieving
Seven seals a-breaking
Six parents wailing
Five distant screams
Four missing kids
Three birch whips
Two clanking chains
and a fire under my Christmas tree

6. The Twelve Days of Krampus

ENGLISH TRADITIONAL FOLK TUNE - WORDS BY FLAT KRAMPUS

Sing sections in the following order:
AB ACDB AC2DB AC3DB AEDB AFEDB AF2EDB AF3ECB AF3EDB AF4EDB AF5EDB AF6EDB AF7EDB
and strive to get it right to avoid the wrath of the Krampus

7. Decked in the Halls

ENGLISH TRADITIONAL FOLK TUNE - WORDS BY FLAT KRAMPUS

Round the streets we run with horns on Fa la la la la la la la la

2. See the Krampus rise before us,
Fa la la *etc.*
Crack the whip and join the chorus,
Fa la la *etc.*
Follow us in vicious measure,
Fa la la *etc.*
Thrashing gives the Krampus pleasure,
Fa la la *etc.*

3. Fast around the Krampus passes,
Fa la la *etc.*
Flee your beating, lads and lasses,
Fa la la *etc.*
Fall we down now all together,
Fa la la *etc.*
Trampled by his boots of leather,
Fa la la *etc.*

8. We Wish You a Scary Christmas

ENGLISH TRADITIONAL FOLK TUNE - WORDS BY FLAT KRAMPUS

Pay no heed to a smirking elf
Put a Krampus on your shelf

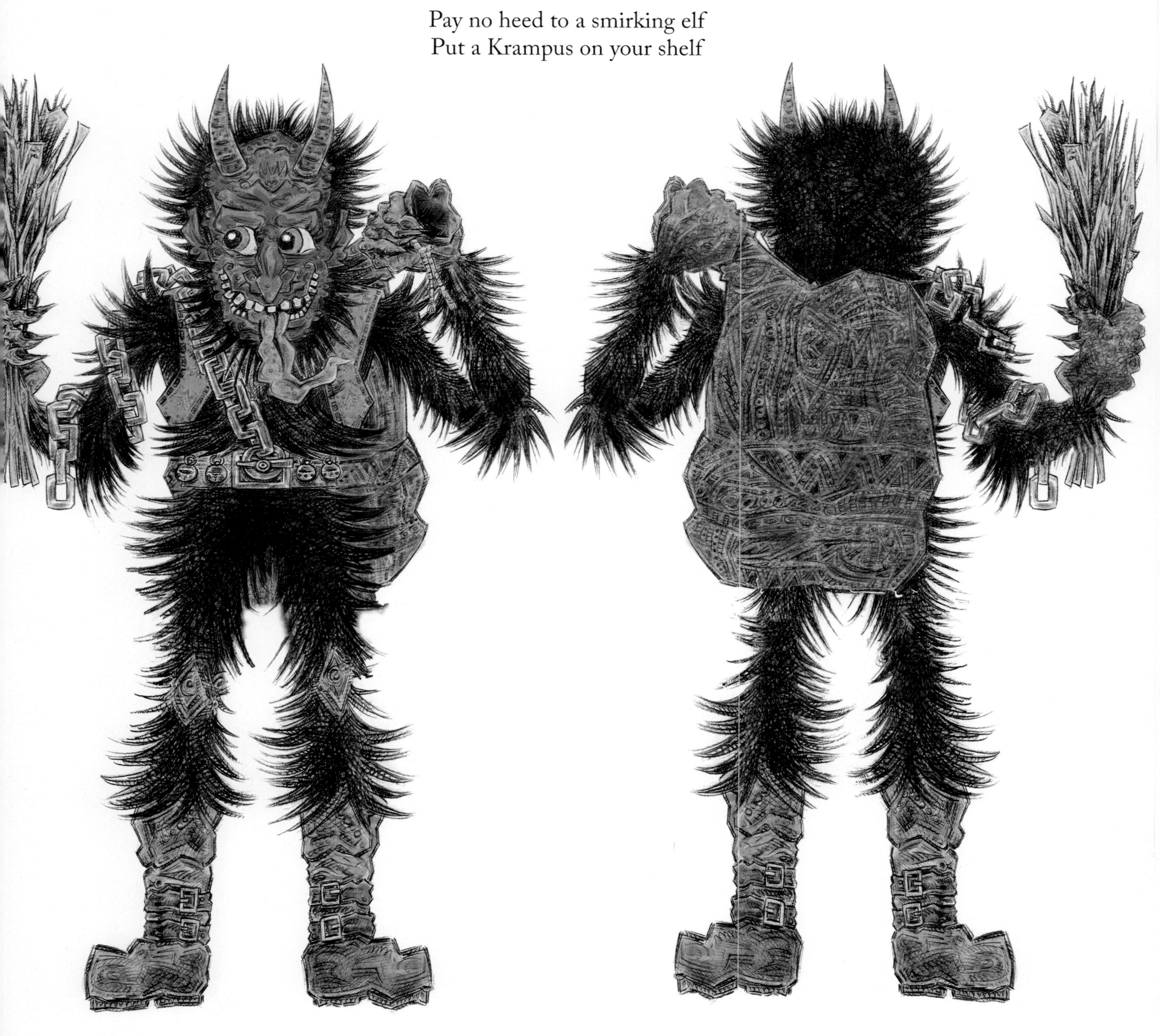

Cut out or copy these Flat Krampus drawings to make a holiday decoration. Fold him at the knee and waist and you can perch him on a shelf or window ledge or computer monitor. Or hang him on your tree with a thread or wire.

Matt Lake (@FlatKrampus) is an award-winning journalist, editor, and writer whose work on *Weird Pennsylvania*, *Weird Maryland*, *Weird England*, and a dozen other books in the Weird book series has kept him on the Naughty list for a more than a decade.

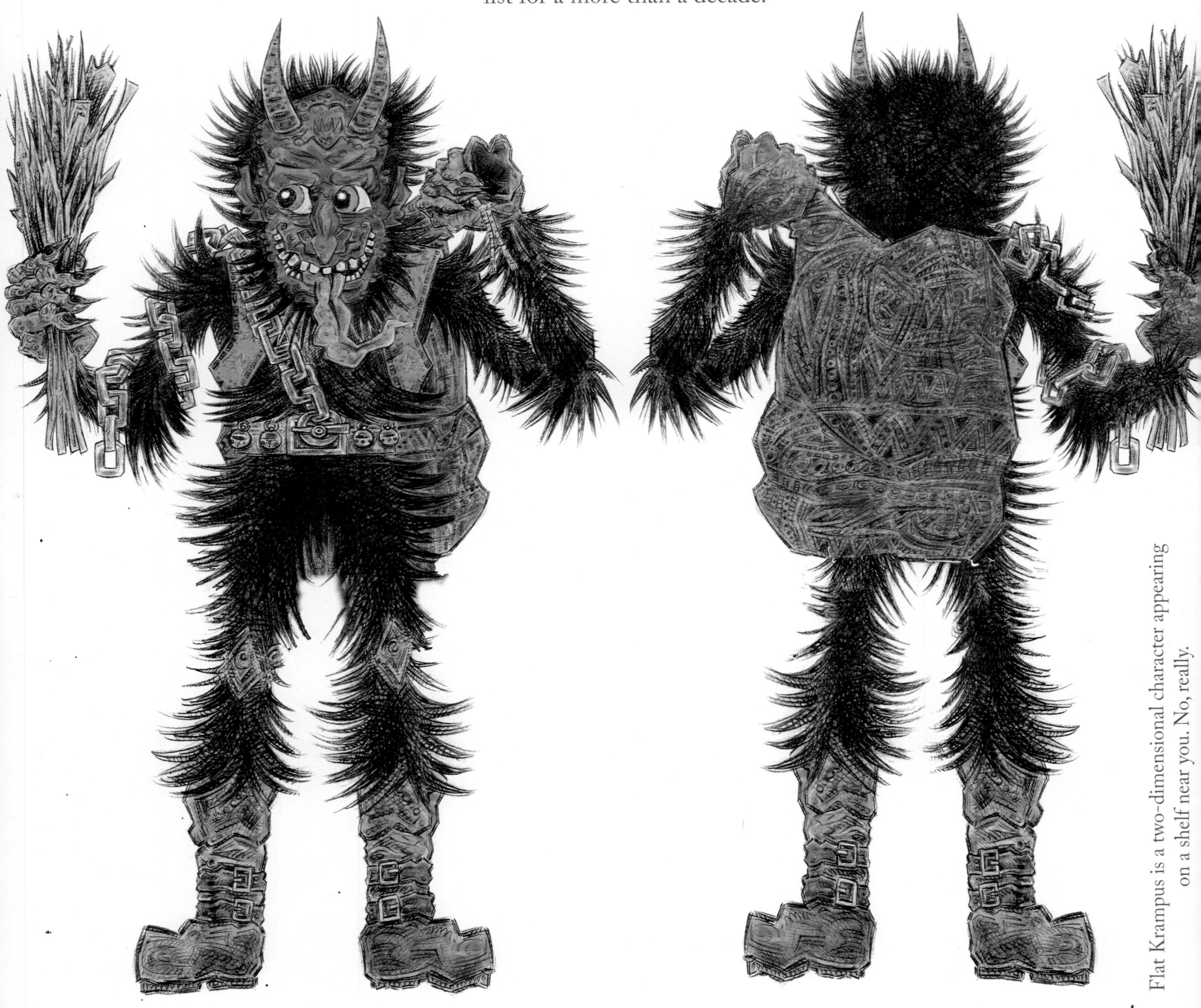

Flat Krampus is a two-dimensional character appearing on a shelf near you. No, really.

James Lincke (@JamesLincke) is a friendly elf-scout whose good cheer has kept him on the Nice list for more than two decades. He writes and acts in a Web series called *The Fun Nun*, based on his graphic novel.